BUILD YOURSELF
HAPPY

BUILD YOURSELF

HAPPY

Written by Abbie Headon

Illustrated by Jenny Edwards

Contents

Foreword: why play?

With the busy pace of modern life, setting aside time for ourselves to relax and be creative is no longer a luxury—it's essential for our health. Research shows that doing a creative activity, even for a short time each day, can positively improve our well-being.

So why play with LEGO® bricks?

You may not have thought about playtime since you were a child, but getting hands-on with LEGO® bricks can help you to reclaim some "me time" and give your mood a boost.

- **Get creative:** Playing with LEGO bricks can help you open your mind to new possibilities and hone your creative skills. It could even make you more likely to come up with innovative solutions in other areas of your life.

- **Learn to collaborate:** Building together with friends and family empowers you to be a strong communicator. You'll naturally share ideas, negotiate rules, and build empathy.

- **Exercise your mind and body:** When you build with LEGO bricks, you use sensory-motor skills that nurture a healthy and active body.

- **Improve your cognitive skills:** With strong cognitive skills, you can solve complex tasks in your life. Building with LEGO bricks can improve your concentration, problem solving, working memory, and flexible thinking.

● **Get in touch with your emotions:** Creativity can be a coping mechanism to help control our emotions. Building with LEGO bricks helps build confidence and self-esteem, and could help you face everyday challenges in life.

● **Practice mindfulness:** What better way to be present in the moment than by concentrating on simple, fun LEGO activities? Mindful activities, such as building with LEGO bricks, can also help you wind down and feel more calm.

Playing with LEGO bricks is certainly not just for kids, so give yourself permission—and the time you need—to take care of yourself and build your way to joy.

About the author

Abbie Headon is an author from Portsmouth, England, who has rediscovered the joy of playing with LEGO bricks. After digging out her childhood collection of LEGO bricks from the attic (and treating herself to a few new sets), she has written this book to help readers unwind, find zen, and build a little bit of LEGO joy into their everyday lives.

Build Yourself Happy

Introduction

Are you failing to find inner peace on a yoga mat? Struggling to decide what box set to watch? Modern life is full of decisions and distractions, and sometimes it's hard to know how we can truly relax and get back in touch with the fun, happy person we are when we're at our best.

 So in this book we're going to look at a truly alternative activity— rediscovering the power of play, with LEGO® bricks!

I have a confession to make: I am not always the most chilled-out person, and I don't meditate every day, even though I have tried it and I know it's good for me. I am a normal(ish) human being who likes reading, eating, and spending too much time on Twitter, and I don't know where all my chakras are.

But I have written a few books on how to live a happier life and I truly believe that there are simple steps we can take to make things a little easier and a lot more fun.

When my editor and I started talking about this project, lots of light bulbs turned on in my head all at once. Yes, I did have a box of LEGO bricks and pieces in the attic from my childhood. No, I hadn't played with it for years. And OH BOY, was I glad to have the chance to rediscover a forgotten channel of joy and creativity.

So I retrieved my old bricks, acquired a few new ones, and reignited a love affair with the LEGO brick. I hope you will, too. We may even become AFOLs (that's "Adult Fans of LEGO") together along the way as we play with our LEGO bricks!

Some people might say that playing is just for kids, but they couldn't be more wrong. Playing is more than just a lot of fun—it brings many real benefits into our lives. It boosts our mood and helps us think more creatively. It helps us develop more positive responses to challenging situations. And having a playful approach to life is also associated with good mental health and well-being.

And you don't just have to take my word for it. Recent research shows that people from all around the world find concrete benefits from creative play: it supports successful learning as adults and children, it builds trust and empathy, and it increases overall happiness levels. So as well as being, well, fun, you could look at LEGO playtime as a form of contemplation; as a welcome distraction from life's more serious demands; and as a means of self-development and building confidence.

You might be a serious grown-up, with adult-shaped responsibilities like paying the rent, going to work, and not running out of milk, but that doesn't mean you have to be serious all the time.

In fact, life would be a little bit grayer and duller if we never made time for fun—and nobody wants that.

In these pages, we'll explore how that childhood favorite, a pile of LEGO bricks, is just as great for adults to play with, and how it can help you find moments of joy that you can carry with you into your daily life.

 You don't need a massive collection. Just a handful of bricks is enough to get started and rediscover the fun of building.

We'll start off with some activities to help us get to know our bricks, then we'll wind things down and find out how we can relax with our LEGO elements. We'll explore the "snap" of joy that LEGO bricks can bring by releasing as much fun and silliness as we can, and discover how LEGO pieces can get us in the mood for sleeping.

After that, we'll get social with a chapter packed with ideas for how you can share the joy of building with friends and family. Then we'll move on to reconnect with our childhood selves. Finally, we'll find out how to make cleaning up more fun, and look at ways to carry the joy of LEGO play with us anywhere we go.

You don't need to be an expert builder to have fun with LEGO elements—take it from me, a very-much-non-expert LEGO builder!

Building with LEGO bricks and pieces is an activity everyone can enjoy, and it's fun and refreshing to do something where the end result isn't the most important thing. You might build something amazing, but the model you create is not what counts here.

 What matters is how you feel when you're building, because you're here to rediscover the joy of play and the process of creating above everything else.

Join me on a journey through the magical, wonderful, joyful world of building with LEGO elements—and find out just how much fun you can have on your own LEGO journey.

Build Yourself Happy

1

Getting started

It's time for some serious fun! Maybe it's been a little while since you last worked with LEGO® bricks, but don't worry—building with LEGO elements is like riding a bike, except that you don't need to wear reflective gear and a helmet. (But you can if that's your style. The bricks don't judge.) Don't be put off if you haven't played with LEGO bricks before—it's never too late to start.

 ## Great news—there's no age limit to LEGO play!

Let's start by checking out the basics so you know what you're working with.

All pieces are welcome here!

You can use any LEGO elements you like. Perhaps you have a box of pieces from your childhood that you can rescue from the attic. Or maybe you can borrow a family member's collection. If your home is currently LEGO free—gasp!—take a look at some of the sets available to buy. They're full of bricks in all different sizes, colors, and shapes.

One of the coolest things about LEGO pieces is that all the elements made since 1955 belong to the LEGO System in Play. This sounds kind of technical but simply means that all pieces fit into the same three-dimensional grid, so you can combine vintage bricks with brand-new ones and they will always fit together.

No matter how many bricks and pieces you've got, you can still have limitless hours of fun. Size isn't important when it comes to your LEGO collection.

 Whether you've got a handful of bricks or a closet full, you can let your imagination run wild and embrace the power of play.

Say "hello" to your bricks

Now that you've gathered up a collection, large or small, it's time to get up close and personal with your pieces. Yes, they all belong to the same system, but each LEGO element is different and special in its own way.

Spread your stash out in front of you, and pick up the pieces one by one. Take a moment to notice all the colors and shapes.

 Run your fingertips over the bumpy studs. Feel the smoothness of their sides, and the textured surfaces of the sloped bricks.

Life isn't black and white, and it's definitely not gray. In fact, it's much more fun when we embrace the full spectrum of colors—the more rainbows, the better! You'll be pleased to know that LEGO bricks come in all sorts of colors, from bold primaries to subtle pastels.

When you look at a brick by itself, you don't know yet what it will become part of—it could be anything! Feel all that potential waiting for it to become a part of something else. Appreciate each piece for what it is. You'll be in the perfect mood for putting those magical pieces together and enjoying the process of connecting brick to brick.

Speaking of connecting pieces, have you heard of "clutch power"? This is the term used to describe the satisfying way that the bricks fasten together—tight enough to stay connected but not so hard that you can't pull them apart again.

 That pleasing "snap" you hear and feel when you connect two bricks? That's clutch power in action!

Make your own LEGO® happy space

I think we can all agree that stepping on a LEGO® element is around pain level nine out of ten—somewhere between "severe" and "worst possible." That's not the happiest feeling in the world so I'll help you get your space organized to avoid treading on those sneaky little studs. Your feet will thank me.

Here are some good places for your LEGO playtime:

- A living room

- A flat surface, such as a desk or dining table

- A portable carry case

- A bookshelf for storage and display—and building if it's at the right height for you.

Maybe you can think of some other places, too?

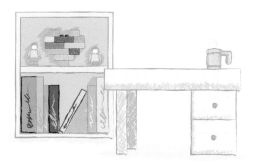

If you're not a child anymore, it's possible you don't have a space in your home that's especially devoted to playtime. If so, don't worry—there are lots of places where you can indulge your LEGO habit.

To avoid your pieces hitting the floor in a "bricksplosion" or, even worse, a "brickvalanche," give yourself as much space as possible, or work inside a tray, box lid, or a cereal bowl. Sometimes those little pieces are just gonna spread their wings and fly, but it's worth trying to keep them in their rightful place if you want to avoid the time-honored hopping-and-shouting dance.

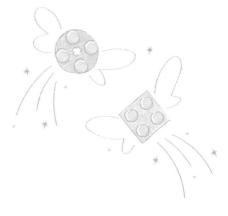

Build Yourself Happy

2

Get into the zone

Whatever happened to doing stuff without a care in the world, like you did when you were little? Whatever happened to just playing and being spontaneous? "Adulting," you'll say. "Adulting happened."

I hear you. No one really wants to grow up and leave all the fun of childhood behind. Somehow, it just happens. But guess what—there is no law to say that playing is just for kids!

If you're like me, however, you might be a bit rusty and stuck on where to begin. Playing "house" isn't fun anymore because we're living it (crying face emoji). People might look at you funny if you start pushing a stroller with a doll in it, and you may well get questioned for throwing water balloons at strangers on Main Street. So how can you start playing again *and* still call yourself a respectable adult?

I'll give you a hint—they snap together and bring happiness to all who get to know them. You guessed it! It's LEGO® bricks. LEGO elements are the perfect tools to help us rediscover the joy of play, because they offer endless possibilities no matter what skill level we have.

Building with LEGO bricks stimulates your creativity in a way that's quite different from your day-to-day routine. It might also take you back to some of your happiest childhood memories spent snapping bricks together.

When you try out some of the ideas in this book, and start inventing your own, you'll find new playful areas of creativity opening up before you. It's very likely that the joy of play will start to spill into other—supposedly more serious—parts of your life, too.

Go with the flow

Unless you're a lottery winner (and if you are, can I please have your number?), you probably can't always get everything you want and that can be pretty annoying. Sometimes, you just have to go with it and snap together the bricks you've been given.

You might remember—or if you're new to LEGO building, then you may have heard—that LEGO sets come with handy booklets, which tell you step-by-step which piece goes where. Now those instruction booklets are incredibly useful if you're aiming to build a LEGO model from a set with all of the specific bricks included in the box.

But what if you don't have a LEGO set? Or you want to simply enjoy the process of snapping bricks together without worrying about what they will become? The best way to unleash your creativity is to let go of the rules.

 This is your time to play, and you can—get this—build whatever you want, however you want!

To get started, spread out your pieces in front of you and connect them without really thinking about what you're making.

As you hold your bricks, give yourself time to feel each one. You might find that certain shapes, sizes, or textures are more pleasing to your senses than others. Start by snapping together the bricks that most appeal to you.

You don't need to make anything specific. Simply enjoy connecting pieces in a totally relaxed way. This will get your creativity going and help you focus on "me time," away from other things in your life.

Without even realizing it, you'll be creating something and giving your mind the space it needs to unleash creativity without a specific aim. How freeing is that?

So much of our lives is directed toward achieving goals, but this time is just for you and your LEGO pieces to get to know each other. So just enjoy it!

Close your eyes

LEGO pieces are fun to look at, with their vibrant colors and shiny surfaces. Just seeing them in my box of bricks makes me want to reach out and hold them. But what if we don't rely on our visual sense for a little while, and take a new approach to LEGO play?

- Arrange a box or tray of pieces close to you, and make sure you have a clear space to work in.

- Close your eyes.

- Feel around gently in your box of bricks and select one LEGO piece. You'll know what shape it is but you won't know what it looks like.

- Take another piece and connect the two LEGO elements. The studs are nice and easy to feel, so this shouldn't be too tricky.

- One by one, add new pieces to your creation.

You'll have a sense of how stable or fragile it is, and you'll feel if it needs a piece added here or there to stop it collapsing. But you won't know much more than this. After you've combined 10 to 12 pieces—or just when you feel like it—put your new build down on the table in front of you, take a breath, and then open your eyes.

What does your new creation look like? Is it anything like what you expected? Would you—could you—have constructed anything like this with your eyes open? Spend a few moments enjoying your creation and admiring its unique and unplannable structure.

 Taking time out from one of our senses is a great way to engage with a new kind of playfulness and reset our minds into a more relaxed mode.

Maybe we don't have to worry about every last little detail all the time, both when we're having fun and in other areas of our lives, too.

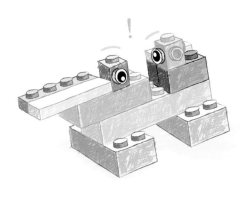

Finding balance

When things aren't balanced, they can come crashing down. It can be scary to think of falling over, but it's usually okay if it does happen. Staying centered and not being pulled too far in one direction of your daily life isn't always easy. And it's the same with LEGO bricks. Just one brick can send your lovely creation toppling over, but on the flip side, one brick can restore balance.

With a little ingenuity we can bring balance back and create builds that can stand on their own two feet (or their own baseplate).

Take a selection of pieces from your LEGO stash, and make a structure that can't possibly stand up by itself. Break all the rules of good building by creating something that has too much weight in one direction.

Next, stand it up and watch it topple over into a resting position. (Don't worry—no LEGO bricks will be harmed during this activity.)

Now see if you can bring it back into balance by adding pieces on the other side, so it can remain standing.

 ## Can you provide this vital support with just one brick?

You might need to play around with the placement of the "balancing brick" (or bricks). Don't worry if it takes a few tries to get it right.

When you build without worrying too much about whether your model can stand up by itself, you allow more possibilities into your LEGO play.

Even if your creation topples over, you have the power to fix it—maybe with just one single "magic brick"! You can carry this powerful LEGO magic into all your future models—and everyday life. You will open yourself up to more creative possibilities by not being afraid to let things fall down.

Spotting your built-in style—and changing it

I have a confession. I am addicted to symmetry. Give me some LEGO bricks—any pieces you've got—and I will make you a symmetrical model.

What I've noticed when I build is that I automatically seek balance and harmony. Without meaning to, I try never to add one piece on its own if I could add two pieces on opposite sides.

Take a look at your creations and notice what kind of thinking is behind their construction. Do you try to match colors or create a house every time you build, for example? What would your builds look like if you stepped outside these rules?

Or maybe you haven't noticed yet. In which case, build two or three small LEGO creations without thinking too hard about what you're aiming for. Are there similarities in what you've built?

 Once you've figured out what your inner guidelines are, make a deliberate choice to ignore them for your next build, and see what happens.

When you make an active choice to try new ways of building, you'll lead your brain into new ways of thinking.

 Trying something new, especially when it comes to creativity, is proven to be beneficial to self-esteem and emotional well-being.

So why not step outside your comfort zone and try building something in a way that wouldn't normally be your go-to style?

Limitless possibilities

You don't need a whole room full of LEGO elements to be able to make almost anything you can imagine. Even with a limited number of pieces, you can make a seemingly infinite number of combinations.

If you have just six 2x4 bricks (bricks that are two studs wide and four studs long), you can connect them in more than 915 million (yes, million!) combinations! So if you have more than six bricks, you can see that the available combinations quickly become astronomical. With even just a shoebox-size collection of LEGO pieces, the building possibilities are (pretty much) endless.

Sometimes, you might feel limited by the options life—or your LEGO collection—has to offer. But if you embrace what you've got and add in a little creativity, you will find that there are more possibilities available than you first thought.

It goes to show that you don't need a whole room full of LEGO bricks to build plenty of awesome creations, expand your creativity, and make you smile.

On the other hand, a whole room of LEGO bricks does sound pretty awesome . . .

Switch 'n' swap

Variety is the spice of life, and sometimes just making a little change can turn things on their heads. Test this theory with LEGO bricks and watch how a simple technique can spice up your building style. It might seem like a small thing, but making just one swap can create a brand-new model. I like to call this "the switcheroo."

Get started by building a little creation—whatever appeals to you today is fine. Personally, I'm feeling like it's a cute little duck kind of day.

Then take two different types of bricks or elements—make sure they are not identical or symmetrical—off your build and swap them. It could be from side to side, from top to bottom, or front to back.

Notice how your LEGO creation changes when you try out "the switcheroo."

 You'll see that even with one tiny change, your creativity can be stretched in new and unexpected directions.

Build Yourself Happy

3

Build to relax

Let's be honest—modern life is busy! So let's take a break from all of the noise and chaos and slow down with some relaxing LEGO® ideas that will help you take a minute to unwind.

Thanks to their bright colors and chunky, varied shapes, LEGO bricks themselves can be relaxing to look at and hold without making anything at all. To some, the idea of making anything with LEGO elements can be daunting, but the ideas in this chapter are meant to keep you feeling chilled out—you don't need a big collection of LEGO bricks or any building skills to relax with your LEGO stash.

If you're up for it, building small models with LEGO elements offers the perfect opportunity to focus in a way that sets our imaginations free, leaving us feeling relaxed, refreshed, and ready for whatever lies ahead.

Just, uh, try not to lose your cool if you keep dropping your pieces on the floor . . .

Turn down the volume

Life can be awfully noisy sometimes. With traffic racing by outside, planes buzzing overhead and other people's music escaping from their headphones on public transportation, it can seem as if we're drowning in a sea of sounds—none of them chosen by us. So it's nice, when we have time to ourselves, to turn the volume down and tune in to the gentle sounds of LEGO bricks snapping together.

First, settle yourself in and get comfy—I'm thinking pajamas, cozy socks, nobody around to bother you, and your phone switched to silent mode (or even better, tucked away where you can't see it). Then, spread out your LEGO stash in front of you, and prepare for a symphony of gentle sounds and sensations.

 Forget about the colors and shapes of the pieces for now. The only thing that we're interested in at this moment is the sound that the pieces make.

Start by swishing your hand through your LEGO collection. Listen to the sounds of the pieces rippling over each other. What does it remind you of? To me, it sounds like waves rolling onto a pebbly beach—I can almost feel those waves lapping over my feet.

Then, pick up two pieces, snap them together and pull them apart. What do you hear? It's a very gentle sound, but with each connection and disconnection you'll hear a distinct "snap," "clunk," or "pop."

 You can close your eyes or keep them open while you join brick to brick and just enjoy the sound of each connection.

Now that you've played with individual connections, build a structure. It doesn't matter what it is, as we're most interested in the sounds right now. Listen to each snap and clunk of the pieces combining. When you're finished, take the pieces apart again, and enjoy hearing them pop back into their separate states once more.

It's all very simple, and not very showy—but sometimes the simplest things in life are the most relaxing, after all. Give yourself permission to dial down the noise in your day and enjoy the sound of LEGO connections being made.

You may have come across ASMR, or "autonomous sensory meridian response" online or in the news. ASMR is a term used to describe the pleasant, tingling sensation some people experience when they hear quiet sounds such as whispers, clicks, tapping, and rustling.

LEGO bricks are perfect for providing these kinds of sensations, from the moment you handle your LEGO box and hear the pieces sliding around inside, to the experience of connecting bricks. Try it for yourself and find out if listening to the sound of LEGO bricks gives you those magical tingles!

Phone-blocker

I love my phone, but I rely on it far too much. I can be permanently connected to the world around me, finding out what people are thinking about, what's in the news, where my friends have been on vacation, what e-mails I'll have to deal with tomorrow . . . it's almost like my phone has become an extension of my hand, and sometimes that can be a real killjoy.

Whenever I could be focusing on the experiences that are actually unfolding all around me, this tiny handheld spoilsport tells me what's happening everywhere else.

 Technology is great, but phones can be relentless.

And having your pocket-sized companion constantly pinging and notifying you about things is a surefire way of interrupting your calming LEGO time.

So, if you want to free yourself from the tyranny of your phone, and you're as short of self-discipline as I am, one of the best ways to do this is with a bespoke LEGO phone-blocker.

The simplest way to put your phone out of service for a little while is to choose one of your bricks—whichever one is looking most in need of a rest—and give it a short vacation from its building work.

Switch your phone into silent mode, put it face down somewhere nearby and gently lay the weary brick on it.

During your LEGO session, you may find yourself thinking, "I'll just check my phone," but then you'll see the snoozing brick and you'll remember to leave it in peace. You know the old saying, after all: let sleeping bricks lie.

As an alternative, if you're feeling really creative, you could build a device to make your phone harder to get to. Whatever works for you to keep you away from all those tempting apps is fine!

Make a pattern

Immersing yourself in a LEGO pattern is a great way to take your mind away from your to-do list. Have you ever looked down from a plane at the fields and towns spread out below you and marveled at the patterns they make on the landscape?

With LEGO bricks you can fly high and make a bird's-eye view with LEGO creations. Also, you won't need to go through passport control or have your bag x-rayed first, which is always a plus.

Shake out your LEGO collection and sort your pieces into groups in which you have two or more of the same kind, so it's easier for you to create patterns. Then, using a clear, flat surface, add pieces one by one, building up a balanced pattern as you go.

You don't need to plan it first—half the fun comes from seeing which pieces spring to your hand and then finding out where they fit best.

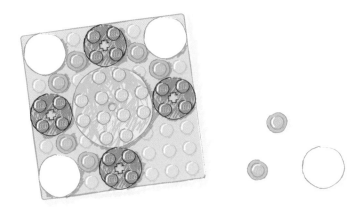

You'll discover that it's a great relaxation and contemplation tool, like doodling—but with bricks!

You can build a flat creation that's all one brick high, or, if you're feeling creative, you can make a build in three dimensions that has several layers, and enjoy seeing how the patterns change and develop with each new layer of intricacy.

Let your mind wander as you select each new group of matching pieces and add them to your build. Take a moment to admire your patterns and feel free to keep adding or swapping colors. The most important thing is to let your mind relax as you create a pattern that's as pleasing to your eye as it is to make.

LEGO® mandala

You've probably seen mandalas before, but did you know that you can make them with LEGO® elements, too?

A mandala is a circular symbol with its origins in Hinduism and Buddhism. It symbolizes the universe in microcosm, and it has also been used by psychologists to represent the concept of wholeness and balance in a person's life. Apart from the deeper meanings we can ascribe to mandalas, they are also beautiful works of art, with symmetry and circular shapes and patterns.

To get yourself in the mandala mood, clear a space and sort your pieces into groups of three or more identical types. Ideally the pieces in each group will be the same color and shape, but if you need to be a little bit flexible, that's fine, too. This is about unwinding, not creating a masterpiece.

This time, we're going to work without clicking the bricks together, meaning that the LEGO elements will slide smoothly over your play surface—and also that they'll need a gentle touch to stay in the right place as you add each new round of pieces. Treating the pieces delicately will allow you time to appreciate each color more fully, and to ease yourself into a more relaxed state of mind as you watch the new patterns growing in front of you.

Starting from a central piece, add circles of LEGO bricks and tiles to create a round structure with a number of rings or branches. If you can include flowers or leafy elements, your mandala might even look like a circular garden.

 Whatever pieces you include, your mandala will be a peaceful abstract design with its own inner beauty.

As you create patterns, watching them grow from a simple starting point to an intricate finished piece, feel a sense of calm and relaxation and enjoy the beauty of the shapes and colors you've arranged into a new creation.

Green fingers (and multicolored bricks)

Is there anything more relaxing than spending time in a peaceful garden, leaning back against a tree trunk and hearing the breeze whisper through the leaves above you?

 Studies show that spending time looking at pictures of nature instantly relaxes us.

And who doesn't need a little more relaxation time? The problem is that even if you have a garden of your own, or a delightful park close by, those good garden vibes can be all too easily ruined by bad weather. So where can you chill out when you can't connect with nature?

With your trusty LEGO kit you can get into the botanical spirit and build a paradise of your very own—one that will flourish even in the depths of winter when everything outside is tightly curled up and waiting for spring to come.

To get into the gardening vibe, go through your LEGO stash and pick out all the pieces in garden colors. Greens and browns are perfect, but you can make your garden or nature build in any colors you like. If you want an all-purple garden, go for it.

Then, conjure up your favorite outdoor space in your imagination and create your very own LEGO garden getaway.

If you have a LEGO baseplate, that's a great starting point for your build. Otherwise, you can build standalone trees and plants. Clusters of flowers can decorate the "grass" in clumps, or maybe they can grow from the top branches of your tree! Don't worry about being too accurate: in a LEGO garden, sea grasses, apples, and transparent lamps all flourish side by side, sometimes even on the same plant.

Take a deep breath and, as you breathe out, bask in the beautiful oasis of calm that you have just created.

Imagine yourself in the space. What do you see? What can you hear? Can you smell blossoms or freshly cut grass? Ah, nature is so relaxing.

Build like no one is watching

"What are you making?" This seems like such a basic and harmless question, but at the same time it can be anything but relaxing. You might not have a clue what you're building, and if it feels like you have to please someone else, the pressure to perform can be immense.

If you're just having fun and exploring your sense of creativity, building a particular "anything" can cramp your style. "Am I doing it right?" you wonder. "Will they know what it is when I've finished?"

So if you want to relax and really enjoy your LEGO time, give yourself a break, turn off your inner critic, and imagine that no one is watching or judging you.

LEGO time is your time, and to be quite frank you can do whatever you like. Nobody is going to take pictures or give you a score. If you're using your phone-blocker, then you might even feel less tempted to take photos of your creations and share them on social media. You don't need the "likes" to love what you build. This is just for you.

This means that you can let go of all those "will it be good enough?" worries and simply do your own thing. Take the pressure off yourself—and the bricks—and simply enjoy the process.

Now that you know the time and space is yours to do whatever you want with, spread out your LEGO pieces and connect them in any way that feels right. Maybe you'll build with no plan at all. Maybe you'll build something that's been tempting you for ages but you've never got around to trying until now. Or maybe you will invent something entirely new that has never been built before—wouldn't that be awesome?

 Let go of expectations, set your creativity free, and let the LEGO magic happen in front of you.

Sometimes the key to relaxation is doing nothing, but the best way to relax is to do your own thing with nothing holding you back. Build it, enjoy it, and relax into pure LEGO creativity.

Build Yourself Happy

4

Build for joy

A little burst of extra joy can make all the difference. Even the snap of brick onto brick can make you smile and add that all-important pop of happiness into your life.

It's often hard to find time to focus on yourself. And making time to dedicate to doing something just because it makes you happy can seem almost self indulgent. But I'm going to stop you before you head down that LEGO® brick road. "Me time" is super important to keep a sense of balance in your life, and it might be just what you need to give you that little extra bit of joy each day.

Playing with LEGO bricks is an easy way to build more happiness into your day by giving yourself time to create and express yourself.

And you don't need to dedicate tons of time to building with LEGO bricks. You can spend as much or as little time as you like playing with them. Whether you play for five minutes or several hours, one thing is for sure—you'll definitely feel a spark of joy by the time you've finished.

So if you feel like you need a little more joy in your life—and let's be honest, who's going to say no to that?—grab your stash of LEGO bricks and get creative.

Things that make you happy

In our busy lives, we rarely allow ourselves enough time to stop and think about the things that really make us happy. Did you know that visualizing happy things will actually boost your mood? And what better way to picture your happy things than with LEGO pieces!

You can build almost *anything* using LEGO elements. Whether you like giraffes, footballs, or ice-cream cones, all you need are some bricks and a healthy dose of imagination to bring them to life. The best part of all? You don't even need to make your build recognizable to anyone other than yourself.

Start by picturing something that makes you happy. Then dive into your brick stash and create something that brings a smile to your face. It can be as simple as a stack of just two bricks in a color that defines happiness for you or a simple build to make you grin.

There's no test at the end and nobody's going to give you a score out of ten, so it doesn't matter if your build doesn't look *exactly* (or even anything) like the object in your mind.

Any time you get your LEGO bricks out, think about having fun and just build what makes you happy!

Unexpected joy

Now on a less joyful note, sometimes two LEGO pieces get stuck together and you can't take them apart again, and this can be a bit frustrating. Please, respect your molars—no using your teeth to pull LEGO bricks apart!

If you don't have a brick separator tool at hand, it's best to just accept that you have a new type of piece now. Perhaps these two pieces were just meant to be together—and you wouldn't want to break up a new romance, would you?

Getting stuck might not immediately sound joyful, but sometimes the unexpected leads us to places we may not otherwise have ended up. Learning to accept that things don't always go the way we planned is a key part of leading a more relaxed life—and our LEGO play is a great place to practice this skill.

The power of colors

Did you know that LEGO pieces have been made in more than 150 colors since the very first bricks appeared in the 1950s? Today, there are still more than 50 colors currently in production, so you have a lot to choose from!

It's no secret that colors affect our moods and energy levels. Colors can help cheer us up, make us feel empowered, and even give us a sense of calm and relaxation.

Shake out your LEGO stash and divide it into different color groups. You'll almost certainly have the six classic LEGO foundation colors: bright red, bright yellow, dark green, bright blue, white, and black. On top of these you will probably have a range of other shades, such as gray, purple, pink, and brown.

Try making builds using different groups of colors to suit your mood. If you feel you need a boost, pick out all the brightest colors in your collection and build something that will make you smile—feel the positive vibes coming out of your eye-popping new creation!

 If you're in a more chill frame of mind, create something using gentler colors such as light pink, gray, white, and beige, which will give off a calmer kind of energy.

Build a rainbow

Sometimes, when the weather is gray and rainy, it's easy to feel that the gloom will last all day . . . and then you look up at the sky and see a huge arc of colors beaming down on you, showing you that every rainstorm ends eventually.

Perhaps the fact that they signal the end of a storm is why rainbows are such a symbol of happiness—along with the fact that they contain all the colors of the—er—rainbow.

If you want to bring some rainbow joy into your LEGO time, why not try building a LEGO rainbow? We can't promise that you'll find a pot of gold at the end of it (though you never know), but what's certain is that you'll feel the joy as you create a beautiful spectrum of LEGO bricks.

Now we all know that a textbook rainbow goes like this: red, orange, yellow, green, blue, indigo, violet. But don't worry if your palette of bricks doesn't quite match this list—in the LEGO universe, you're allowed to take liberties with color science. (Some of us just can't get enough blue bricks, for instance.)

 It's your rainbow, so you can do it your way!

Sort your bricks into a rainbow selection—either meteorologically sound or your own version of the spectrum—and then see where your creativity leads you. You may have to be a little inventive about how your rainbow connects if some of your bricks are different sizes and shapes, but you'll find your own way.

Your rainbow doesn't have to be formed in a scientific arc either. You might find yourself building a rainbow tower, a rainbow cube, or a rainbow road for your minifigures to frolic along. Whichever direction you build in, you're sure to feel sunny along the way, and open your mind to a whole spectrum of ideas.

Pick a palette

Modern life often tells us that "more" is the solution to all our problems: more belongings, more flavors, more TV channels. But sometimes we can find real happiness when we try "less" for a little while.

When you cook with just a few ingredients, for example, the result can be just as delicious as when you use a whole shopping cart of flavors. In fact, it's often better, because you can focus on the individual elements.

So in this activity, you're going to focus on a single color and limit your pool of bricks to just one shade. Start by dumping your brick stash out in front of you, and separate out all the bricks of a particular color. Now let's see what happens when you focus on that single color.

 It can be any color you like, whether that's sunshiny yellow, grass green, or whatever hue feels most like "you" today.

So, using just this set of matching bricks, set your imagination free and see what your creativity produces!

You may find that this limited selection of pieces presents you with combinations you wouldn't normally choose, such as pieces with sticking-out sidebars or plates with smooth curved surfaces—and because of this, you'll be making new connections and inventing new models before you know it.

Once you've tried this technique with one color, spend a while working through the rest of your stash, until you've created a host of brand-new, perfectly matched creations. Some of your models may be tiny, if you have only a few bricks in that color—but that will just stretch your creativity levels to new heights. And yes, you are allowed to build a tree entirely out of blue bricks if you want to.

 When you start expressing yourself through color, you may find yourself expressing so much more besides.

And once you've finished your one-color building, you'll go out into the world ready to seize the maximum potential with whatever ingredients your day gives you.

Visualize your happy place

It might be a rainy Wednesday or a sleepy Sunday but don't worry—with LEGO bricks you can create a representation of the place where you want to be and pretend you're there. The only limit to where you can go is your imagination.

Perhaps you dream of jetting off on an exotic holiday. Maybe you're missing a loved one and want to build yourselves together at your favorite place. Or you may be happiest at home or around your own town or city. Sometimes joy isn't far away, but just around the corner. You could choose somewhere nearby or a faraway spot that makes you smile just thinking about it.

 When you picture your happy place, you can imagine yourself being there.

Wish you were here!
X

The thought of building a big, complex model might make you feel anything but joyful. You don't have to build your happy place how it looks in real life. Instead, maybe snap a few bricks together while you think of your happy place. Every time you look at what you've made, you'll be reminded of your happy place and you can picture yourself being there.

If it's a place you want to visit again and again, keep your creation somewhere you can see it when you need a little joy in your day. Transport yourself there in your mind, and the model will instantly lift your spirits every time you set eyes on it.

In your dreams

You probably have lots of dreams. Not those weird ones where you go to school in your underwear—dreams of what you want to achieve in your life. There's not much that's more joyful than making your dreams come true, is there?

When you build your dreams using LEGO bricks, you allow those thoughts to become more real to you.

And seeing your dreams take shape will unlock more joy in your life, making the journey toward your goals a little bit easier and more fun.

 When your ambitions are unleashed into the universe, there's nothing stopping you from achieving them!

Maybe the goal you're aiming for is right there at the front of your mind, or maybe your ambitions are buried a little deeper. If it's the latter, you could start by writing down some things that matter to you to see if they bring out any goals that might be hiding in the crevices of your mind (not unlike those sneaky 1x1 pieces that are somehow always lurking in the corner of the sofa).

Either way, take a moment (or longer) to think about what you'd like to achieve, and then create a vision of it using bricks from your LEGO collection.

It can be anything you want—from learning a musical instrument to traveling the globe. And you can create as many dreams as you want any time you want to. No dream is too big or too small, and all you need is a few bricks to build it. Don't worry if your dream seems hard to make using LEGO pieces. It doesn't have to be a big model. A group of three bricks makes a fine mountain. It's all about the idea of building your dream to make it seem real and achievable to you. Saying that, if you want to build a full scale Mount Everest, go for it! You might need a few more bricks though . . .

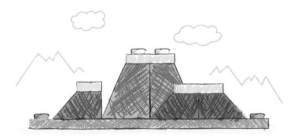

At the end of your building session, you don't have to break up your model and put all your bricks away. If you've built something that represents a key goal you want to conquer, you can keep your build and look at it every day to remind yourself of where you want to be.

Seeing your dreams built before you will remind you that you can achieve them because, after all, you've already made them.

Towering ambitions

Take your LEGO fun to new heights by building a tower that would put the Empire State Building, the Shard, or the Petronas Towers in the shade. With a little ingenuity you'll be amazed just how high you can go.

There's just one rule: the only way is up. How you get there is up to you. It all depends on your "Builder Personality":

- **The Wise Builder:** Builds are attached to a baseplate, because a solid foundation is the best way to succeed.

- **The Daring Builder:** Towers go up, but they can also reach out to the sides, defying gravity and all the rules of physics.

- **The One-Track-Mind Builder:** Every layer is the same size: yep, right from the very bottom to the very top. Consistency is key!

- **The Designer:** A tower just isn't complete until it has a balcony and a helicopter landing pad for visiting minifigures, really.

Release your inner architect and enjoy the view from the top of your new creation!

It might take you some time to figure out your "Builder Personality" or how high you can actually go while keeping your tower stable. But this is a process. Try out different builder styles to see which one suits you the best.

It's okay to let your tower fall over. And it's totally fine to deconstruct it if you don't like how things are going. Just take a deep breath, remember that it's normal for things to go wrong sometimes, and start over. The bricks don't mind how long it takes.

 Building as high as you can go will inspire confidence, filling you up with pride and, most importantly, joy.

I like to move brick, move brick

What is more joyful than the feeling of whooshing through the park on a bike? Or going for a leisurely Sunday drive through the countryside. Sometimes we travel in a vehicle purely because we enjoy the feeling of motion.

 Not only do we enjoy the actual journey, but we also love the feeling of movement, of moving forward.

Traveling to the dentist aside (you haven't been using your teeth to pull bricks apart instead of your brick separator tool, have you?), when we travel, we are often going somewhere we really want to be, whether it's a long-awaited vacation, a trip to LEGOLAND® Park (come on, you know you want to), or a visit to those we love most dearly. We are moving toward joy and you can do the same with your LEGO builds.

LEGO bricks are, of course, stationary, but they can move when you add wheels. You don't have to build a vehicle. You can add wheels to anything like a "wheely" cute bird or giraffe. (Sorry. Okay, not sorry.)

Once your wheels are attached—even just to a single brick—glide your model along the surface in front of you. Envision yourself moving forward toward joyfulness.

Can you remember being a child and enjoying the sensation of pushing a toy car? Rediscover that joy when you grip your LEGO wheels on your play surface. Feel the smoothness of the model rolling along and just appreciate the feeling of movement in your hand, traveling up your arm and making you feel like you're really going places.

Build Yourself Happy

5

Builds to help
you sleep

This might sound surprising, but the same LEGO® bricks that make you feel so full of fun and energy during the day can make you feel much calmer and quieter at bedtime. This means they're perfect for helping you chill out and get in the mood for sleep. Playing peacefully with LEGO bricks gives you screen-free time to relax after a busy day and set yourself up for a restful night.

 At first glance, it might seem that "playing" is not the most obvious way to get ready to sleep.

But these LEGO activities will help you to disconnect from the frenetic pace of the day, so that you're ready to sleep well and begin tomorrow with a spring in your step. And you can use your LEGO bricks to create a cozy atmosphere and start a new bedtime routine.

Establish a routine

With our busy lives, it can be difficult to switch off at night and ensure we get enough sleep. But getting adequate sleep is key to our emotional and physical well-being.

 Studies show that having a bedtime routine reminds our bodies that it's time to wind down and go to sleep. This could make it easier for us to fall asleep.

And let's be honest, who doesn't want more sleep?

Doing a calming activity before bed is also shown to help us unwind and get ready for sleep, so why not incorporate LEGO play into your bedtime routine? You can spend as much or as little time as you like before bed—preferably in a quiet room with low lighting—playing with LEGO bricks.

When you're feeling relaxed, head to bed and get the good night's sleep you deserve.

A note on screens

We all love scrolling through our phones and tablets, checking out the latest cat memes and liking friends' photos on social media. Watching TV before bed is something a lot of us do, too.

 However, sleep experts recommend switching off screens at least 30 minutes before bedtime.

The blue light emitted from our screens can interrupt our bodies' production of a sleep hormone called melatonin, which means we won't sleep as well.

I'm not suggesting you sit in silence before bed. That would not be very relaxing for many of us! There are lots of other calming things you can do, such as reading, doodling, and of course building with LEGO bricks.

So switch off that screen, have a stretch, and give yourself permission to play with your LEGO collection before bed.

Set a time limit

After we've grown up, we don't often have a parent or other authority figure telling us it's time for lights out. As annoying as that was when we were growing up, they had our best interests at heart.

 One key to getting a good night's sleep is to try to go to bed around the same time every night.

Playing with your LEGO collection is obviously fun, and if I'm honest I could spend hours unwinding with my bricks before bed. But it would not be good for sleep if I got carried away and spent every night building until the wee small hours of the morning.

To avoid your LEGO fun interrupting your restorative sleep time, give yourself a time limit so that you'll know when to send yourself—and your bricks—off to dreamland.

Bedtime kit

What's on your bedside table at the moment? If you're anything like me, there's a pile of books waiting to be read, your cell phone, perhaps a photograph. This stuff is all very useful and good, but without a bedside LEGO box or bowl, your nightstand is incomplete—trust me on this.

 Connecting LEGO bricks is a wonderful way to divert your mind away from the scurrying thoughts about today's events and tomorrow's tasks.

So why wouldn't you want to keep a collection of LEGO bricks close by your bed to help you forget about the worries of your day and prepare for a great night's sleep?

To make the perfect LEGO bedtime kit, you will need:

- **A small selection of LEGO bricks:** around ten would be ideal, and it's best if they're chunky bricks, as these will be easier to find than tiny ones if they get lost in the covers. Choose whichever colors you find most restful. You might like to have them all the same color or all pale, calming colors—whatever works for you is perfect.

- **A container to keep them in:** such as a small lunch box or food storage container. (Ideally, if you can, use something that seals shut so the pieces won't fly out if you accidentally knock your kit over when you get up in the morning.)

- **A shallow tray for building in:** with a lip around the edge—a shoebox lid is ideal, if you have one, or it could be the lid of the container you keep your bricks in.

Then carve out some space on your bedside table so you'll see your bedtime LEGO set every time you get ready to hit the hay. When you get into bed, spend as much time as you like connecting your bricks, allowing any worries of the day to drift away as you build. You can make something specific or just enjoy the connections and disconnections.

 Feel yourself relaxing more and more as you play, until it's time to put your LEGO box away for the night and go to sleep.

Together and apart

Sometimes, all you need is the easiest of all possible LEGO activities to put you in the mood for sleeping. This activity will help you wind down from all the excitement of the day and get ready to rest thanks to the power of repetitive building and dismantling.

Choose a selection of bricks—it could be just three or four nice chunky pieces, or a small handful of your favorites. Without thinking too hard about it, connect them together into a structure, and then take them apart again. Repeat as many times as you like, either making the same build every time or creating different variations depending on which piece comes next to your hands.

As you build and dismantle your creation, allow your mind to relax a little bit more each time.

Focusing your attention on these physical sensations will help you let go of the stresses of the day, because there's nothing specific you have to achieve here—just rhythmically moving the pieces together and taking them apart is enough.

If you've had a stressful day, you can imagine that the bricks represent something that has been troubling you.

By dismantling your problems and building their parts into something more satisfying, you might feel like you can put the day behind you and drift off to sleep with ease.

After a while, when you're feeling nice and sleepy—or when you've reached your set bedtime—tuck your bricks safely away into their container and then ease into bed for a peaceful night's rest.

Imagine a happy dreamland

For a gentler entry into sleep-time, try building yourself a peaceful scene and sending yourself there in your mind, far away from the cares of the day.

It could be a gentle landscape with trees and flowers; a golden, sandy beach; or even a plane to fly you away to dreamland. Allow yourself to focus fully on the experience of building—the sounds, the feel of the bricks in your fingers, your ideas about which brick to attach next.

 Without even trying, you'll find yourself feeling much more relaxed and ready to swap the worries of daily life for sweet dreams and restful sleep.

If you don't feel like building something complicated, you could even attach some LEGO flowers and seaweed pieces to a LEGO plate and imagine it's your favorite peaceful place.

Once you've finished your creation, close your eyes and picture the scene you've created. Tune out the sounds around you, or transform them into a part of your relaxing scene. A ticking clock could become the soft drops of rain in a peaceful, leafy jungle.

Picture yourself there. Take three deep breaths. What does it smell like? Is there a breeze? Let your scene fill up your senses as you imagine yourself in this calm oasis.

Then put your build away and let yourself drift off to sleep, thinking of this most relaxing landscape. Ahh . . .

6

Connecting pieces, connecting friends

Spending time with our families and friends can bring huge benefits to our emotional well-being, taking our minds off our worries and giving us a boost that stays with us for days.

Sharing a LEGO® experience is a positive and creative way to connect with those dearest to you. Enjoy the fun and games of playing with LEGO elements just like you did as a kid. But try to keep sibling rivalry to a minimum—that means you, hair-pulling little brothers!

When you take time to enjoy LEGO activities with friends and loved ones, the creative play of building with colorful bricks sparks new conversations and stimulates fun new ways of thinking. This bonding time will leave you all feeling calmer, happier, and ready to build new connections in your everyday life.

Sharing time, sharing pieces

 There's only one thing that's more fun than playing with LEGO bricks by yourself, and that's playing with LEGO bricks with your friends.

Now that you've (re)discovered the joy of creating with LEGO bricks, friends and family in your life will thank you for sharing it with them. Who knows, they may already be LEGO fans, and they just haven't told you yet!

We hear on the news all the time that people live too much of their lives in front of screens, socializing online rather than in person. By doing this, we are missing that feeling of connection we get when we are physically in the same room with friends. While these headlines may not tell the whole story, it's certainly true that spending time together, in person, is a great way to relax and deepen our friendships.

When you take time to simply be with one another, chatting about life's ups and downs with no screens in sight, your connections will grow stronger, and you'll be able to focus on each other's stories without being distracted by the ping of your cell phones or whatever's on the TV. What better way to connect with friends and family than by connecting LEGO bricks together?

You don't need any special preparations for a shared LEGO session. Simply pile your bricks—just a handful will do—in the center of the table and invite your family or friends to connect LEGO pieces as you all talk about the day's events. It doesn't matter what you build. The important thing is to spend time together doing something you all enjoy.

You may find that the builds you create trigger new ideas and subjects of conversation, or the process of building may simply occupy your hands and senses in a way that allows your attention to rest gently with your co-builders, without feeling too intense.

 Sometimes just holding LEGO pieces and playing with them helps you become more focused and engaged in the conversation than you might usually be.

There's something very happy-making about having a shared endeavor—you could even say that LEGO bricks help build friendships as well as spaceships!

Piece it together

The idea of "team building" might make you cringe. But by sharing a fun activity, you really can connect with others in a happy and surprising way.

Gather a small group of people you already know or want to get to know better—they could be friends, roommates, family members, or colleagues—and sit around a table with your brick stash in the middle where all of you can reach it. Even a space on the floor will work.

To start, pick a lucky person to connect two bricks, and then take turns, going around the group, to add a piece to your shared creation, and just wait and see what amazing result you come up with as a team. You can start with a shared target if you want to—like building a house, a car, or a crazy creature—but it's just as much fun to build without a plan and see what emerges.

Collaborating on a shared, low-stakes project like this is a really helpful way not just to build our friendships, but also to reinforce the skills of cooperation that we need in our everyday lives.

 It's a lot of fun to see what happens when several imaginations come together to create something totally unique.

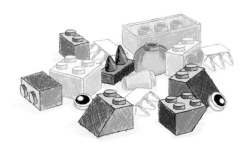

Story collab

From the fairy tales we read as children to the shows we binge on as so-called adults, we all love a good story—and the more thrilling, the better. But we don't have to limit ourselves to absorbing other people's stories—it's actually lots of fun to create our own, especially when we do it with other people.

Building a LEGO story is a perfect way to while away an afternoon or an evening with friends. It's also a lot cheaper than going out for cocktails at that new place in town, and your head won't hurt the next day either—so what's not to like?

With a small group (three to five is ideal), start by dumping out your collection of bricks. It can be a handful or a heap.

Give everyone ten minutes to build something using bricks from the central shared stash. It can be literally anything, such as a house, a wall, a vehicle, a mountain, an animal, or a ULO (that's an "unidentified LEGO object," of course).

Decide who will start the story. This person places their build on the table and begins the story, explaining with a few sentences what it is and why it's important. If you have a minifigure or two who can be the main characters of the story, that's great—but if not, you can improvise with something else—or maybe the new builds will be characters themselves.

When the first storyteller has set the scene, their neighbor picks up the tale and explains what happens next, and you continue moving the story from person to person, adding new information each time.

 As the story unfolds, you'll find your group creativity takes you to unexpected places that each of you would never have found working alone.

And you may find yourselves building new creations to add to the story—new monsters, new challenges, new heroes, and more.

When the story is finished, look at what you've created together and relish in your collective creativity. You'll learn more about yourself and your friends—and how awesome multiple creative minds can be when it comes to making up stories and building together.

You may find that your story and model have become so interesting and involved that you want to meet up and build on the idea again. If this happens, make a note of where you've got to, or take a few key update photos on your phones and arrange to pick up the story again next time. Who needs box sets when bricks are this exciting?

Speedy challenge

They say we're all time-poor these days, though I have a sneaky suspicion that if we spent a little less time online, a whole bunch of useful hours would magically appear. In any case, if, like me, you find yourself pressed for time, you can still squeeze in some excellent, fast-paced LEGO fun with friends and family.

When you and a friend or two find yourselves with a few spare minutes and a handy stash of LEGO pieces nearby, you're perfectly set up for a high-octane game of speed-builds.

Set a timer for one minute, and as the countdown starts, challenge your fellow builders to piece together the LEGO elements right in front of you.

Feel the adrenaline pumping as your brain and fingers strive to create a finished build while the clock ticks down—it's certainly a great way to focus your attention and be fully in the moment, and a little healthy competition is no bad thing either.

When the clock reaches zero, compare your builds as a group and enjoy looking at what you've created as each person tries to guess what each little model could be. Some of the guesses are sure to have you doubled over with laughter—and I think we can all make time for that!

If you enjoy a speed challenge, there are lots of different ways to play. Here are a few more ideas to get you going:

- Increase or decrease the time limit—what can you build in five minutes or 30 seconds?

- Set a target of how many bricks to use—for example, at least ten or no more than five.

- Challenge your friends to build something specific (but not complicated!) in a minute or a few minutes.

It's amazing what you can create in just seconds and with a few LEGO bricks. You'll not only find out how your friends work under pressure but you'll also have a chance to appreciate each other's personal styles.

It's as easy as A,B,C

For another twist on shared LEGO play, invite your friends to a round of "The Alphabet Game." In this activity, you each build something that starts with the same letter, and then the other players have to guess what you've built. So, starting with the letter "A," members of the group might build their LEGO versions of an apple, an anaconda, an alligator, or (hello, fellow punctuation geeks) an apostrophe. The builder can collect points for each correctly identified item, or just enjoy the challenge and move on to the next round.

 It's your game, so you can play it however you want to.

Some people might want to go all out with a fancy model. But it's more than likely that the joy in the game will come from the funny models that most people come up with!

If you find yourself with duplicate builds, you can either reward your players for their synchronised thinking with an extra point, or decide that it's the duplicate builders' turn to provide the next round of snacks.

Carry on through the alphabet until you run out of time or make it to the end (and meet a fleet of LEGO yachts filled with xylophone-playing zebras!). Whatever happens, your creativity and imagination will get a serious workout, and you'll all have lots of fun along the way.

Getting to know you

As well as being great for high-energy, creative fun, LEGO play can give us a wonderful way to express our more thoughtful selves, and this makes it ideal for helping us get to know each other better. If you've ever struggled to put your thoughts into words, you may discover that a handful of bricks gives you a new way to share your ideas with those who are closest to you—or reconnect after some time spent apart.

Get together with a small group of friends, or even just one close friend, and make yourselves comfortable. Choose one of the following techniques and let LEGO bricks help you connect on a new level.

- **Building my story:** Each person takes bricks from the pool of LEGO pieces in the middle of the table and builds something that represents them. When everyone has a finished creation, take turns to listen to the story behind each build, and ask questions to find out more about each person's story.

  It can be as simple as one colored tile, for example—if you want to describe a favorite color—or a single element such as a jewel if you want to let everyone know how much you love a treasured possession.

  This activity is about listening and getting to know each other better. You don't have to add to your friends' stories or builds. Sometimes, just listening and being there is enough. Let the pieces inspire each person to share something about themselves.

Connecting pieces, connecting friends

 You're my fave-brick: Take a few bricks—five or six is plenty—and piece together a small model that makes you think of one of the friends you're with. Then share your thoughts with your friends. It can be a super simple model and it doesn't have to look like anything, since you'll be describing what it is. The point is to think about your friends—new or old—and make something that reminds you of them.

Using your bricks to help share fun memories with friends will make the connections between you and your friends even stronger.

LEGO® night in

We all know what it's like to feel overwhelmed with choice. It's easy to spend hours with friends during an otherwise carefree night in, watching countless Netflix trailers without actually choosing a show to watch.

Next time you and your friends, family, or significant other plan a night in, why not skip the TV drama and play with your LEGO® stash instead?

 All you need for this fun night in is five or six bricks. Sometimes less really is more, and by limiting our choices we can limit distractions and open ourselves to creativity.

Set out up to six bricks for each person. Connect your bricks as you chat about your week—and even your favorite TV shows. After a few minutes, admire each other's creations; enjoy laughing at them and discussing your mini creations.

Next, how about some crazy LEGO challenges to bring a party feel to the evening? Here are some suggestions for fun LEGO games to play with your friends or family:

- **Think of three models to build blindfolded.** Everyone in the room should build the same thing. Open your eyes. What do the models look like? Whose is the funniest?

- **Who can build the best model with the fewest bricks?** Challenge your neighbor!

- **Create some models using only your thumbs.** Or perhaps with just one hand?

- **Guess the number of bricks in the pile.** Whose guess is the most accurate?

- **Make a giant LEGO pizza.** Add lots of incredible toppings!

Connecting online

We know that face-to-face time is better than FaceTime in an ideal world—but sometimes life takes us far from our friends, and we have to rely on technology to help us stay connected. It may seem hard to believe at first, but our gadgets can actually bring us together for shared LEGO fun, even when we can't get together in person over a brick stash.

Thanks to apps and social media, we have the option to link up over live video and share our experiences in real time.

 So, instead of just talking, why not line up your bricks and do some long-distance building?

With a friend or family member who has access to a small LEGO stash, arrange a time when you can both chill out with your bricks. Then set up your phone, tablet, or laptop so the camera can see you and your building space. Dial up your building buddy, and while you're chatting, piece together your LEGO bricks. You might carry on a whole conversation just snapping bricks—not thinking about what you're building but feeling more connected to one another as you join together each LEGO element. Or you might want to share building ideas and admire the other person's creations as you talk.

Meeting up with our BFFs (that's "Building Friends Forever," of course) for LEGO fun is a fabulous way to enjoy playing together with all the joy of childhood, however old we are. By creating something together, even though you might be thousands of miles apart, you'll feel more connected—and who doesn't want to feel a little bit closer to a friend or family member they're missing?

You could even keep your mini creation somewhere you can see it to remind you of that person when you can't talk or be together. The next time you chat with that person online, pick up your build and create something new!

Build Yourself Happy

7

Be a child again

"Stop being so silly and grow up!" is a phrase I remember exasperated teachers using when I was a child, and it seems to me that we spend a lot of our childhoods being asked to be older than we are. So it's only fair that when we actually are grown up, we should reclaim our right to be young and release our inner children once more.*

In this chapter, we'll reconnect with our younger selves and have fun with some anything-goes activities. As we grow up, we sometimes forget to give ourselves time to play, but letting a little silliness into our lives can help us feel more energized and creative—and ready to take on the serious business of adulting once again.

When we rediscover the pleasures of childhood, we open up new possibilities in all aspects of our lives. Play releases tension and induces laughter—which is surely one of the best ways to achieve a happy approach to life. Go on, embrace your "kidult" side.

*Does not apply to all aspects of life. It might be weird if you threw a tantrum over who gets to sit in which seat in the car.

Think like a kid

Kids can be weird sometimes. If you don't believe me, just think back to your own childhood for a minute. Some highlights of mine included leaving my teddy bear in the woods to commune with the other bears who lived there (we never saw him again, so maybe I was right?), setting up a shop under the stairs to sell my family's own belongings to them, and eating carrots sliced only the right way (in delicious sticks and not in round disks of pure wrongness).

 Children see the world differently from us grown-ups, because their expectations about how things "should be" haven't solidified yet.

Remember when a blanket could be a tent, an ocean, or the sky? It didn't just have to be a boring thing that went on the bed. If we introduce a bit of this off-the-wall logic to our LEGO® play, we're bound to make interesting new discoveries, and maybe we'll start to see other parts of our lives differently, too. You could call it thinking outside the LEGO box.

Next time you're settling down for a LEGO session, give yourself permission to let your imagination run riot, just like you used to do when you were little. As you pick up each LEGO piece, feel its potential to be literally anything, and connect it to its fellow pieces with this spirit of freedom in mind.

Maybe, for example, you'd like to build a little house—but then the house sprouts wheels or shoots up on tall legs. Or perhaps you've built an animal (a new species, never before seen by biologists!), and you find it has flowers growing on its head.

When you give yourself the freedom to create things that don't make sense from a grown-up's point of view, you start to see the world in new ways.

 And with this fresh way of looking at life, you may start to find new solutions to the challenges you face beyond your LEGO playtime, too.

School's out!

Remember when you were a kid and school was canceled unexpectedly because of bad weather or a flood in the school gym? You had the freedom to play with whatever you wanted for a whole day, and I bet you didn't spend the day worrying about tomorrow's work. You just dived into the surprise gift of a day of fun, with no reservations.

As adults, it's easy to squander the bonus helpings of free time that come our way by sinking into our phone, staring at our laptop, or fretting about all the things we need to do. But life could be so much more fun than this.

 If we grabbed the random chunks of freedom that come to us and used them in a positive way, we'd feel more refreshed and happier when normal service resumes and it's time to pick up again.

Next time you have an unexpected delay or cancellation—say, the delivery people are running late and you're stuck at home with nothing to do, or you can't get to the store until the snow melts—instead of letting this free time slip away, use it as an opportunity for some LEGO "me time."

Make it up as you go

Goals, targets, destinations—a lot of grown-up life is focused on getting to a particular point by a particular time. Whether it's a task at work, a recipe (oh no—we've run out of eggs!), or even planning something fun like a trip to the movies, there are lots of stages and there's a very clear result that we're aiming for.

And that's fine, I suppose—it certainly gets stuff done, and often organization is essential. But it can be a lot of fun to live without a plan sometimes, and playing with LEGO bricks can be a great way to try this out.

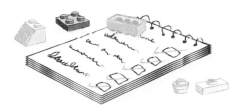

Try throwing all your cautious planning instincts to the wind, and allow yourself to choose and connect bricks without thinking about where you're going or what the finished result will be. You'll be surprised at what you create—and your internal planner/worrier/killjoy may realize that it can let go more often as a result.

When you turn off your inner critic's running commentary, you can enjoy the sheer pleasure of creation, just like the kid you used to be.

Playing like a kid could be the perfect way to rediscover the calmer, fun-loving you that sometimes gets squashed under all those plans and deadlines.

Try something new

If I asked you to try something new, right now, and with no preparation, how do you think you'd handle it? Your heart might start beating faster as you worry about what I might ask you to do. But remember when we were kids? Our hearts were pumping then, too, but with excitement and anticipation of what the unknown could bring.

Sometimes we fall into a habit of forward-planning and risk-avoidance which means we forget the fun of trying new things—and when this happens, we leave our childhood selves behind, wondering where all the fun went.

During our childhood, parents, teachers, and friends were always inviting us to try something new, and we would just go for it. It could be unpleasant (broccoli), tricky (chopsticks), exciting (Bunsen burner), or scary (top bar of the jungle gym), but every day brought such an onslaught of new experiences that we just went with the flow, taking each one as it came.

 Use your LEGO time to reconnect with your sense of adventure and newness.

Experience the fun of testing limits and making something that's new to you.

Maybe you'll think "I've never built a bug zapper/penguin/disco ball before" and just go for it, without worrying too much about how it's going to come together.

Kids don't care if other people can't "see" what the LEGO model they've made looks like and whether it's even close to what it "should" be in real life—or if it is indeed something that exists in the real world. With a healthy dose of confidence, a child might say, "That is NOT a box. It's a treasure chest, silly!"

 When you open your mind to new experiences you'll find that the world becomes a bigger, more interesting place, full of possibilities.

Your LEGO playtime is a great place to start—you never know where this kind of thinking might take you! And you don't even have to eat broccoli along the way if you don't want to.

Get an adrenaline rush!

Time to get an adrenaline rush! Embracing a challenge and discovering what you can achieve is a truly joyful feeling.

Some people perform better under pressure and actually enjoy the sensation of adrenaline coursing through their veins. If this sounds like you, read on. However, if the very thought of building to a deadline makes you feel as unstable as a tower with no "clutch power," then maybe skip this one. After all, you should only be doing things that fill you with joy, not with dread!

Grab your LEGO stash and open up a stopwatch app; find a timer from an old board game; use the timer on your oven or microwave; or find a good old-fashioned alarm clock, if you're fully committed to analog. Now give yourself a minute—yes, just 60 seconds—to make a build.

Your creation can be something completely original, or you can set yourself the challenge of making a particular object, like a car or a cat. The only rule is that when your 60 seconds are up, you have to stop. Can you finish your masterpiece before the alarm goes? Only time will tell.

If you love the buzz of building under pressure like this, you could up the stakes by setting yourself a longer time, with a challenge of using ALL the pieces in front of you.

How many things can you build before the time runs out? And who knows what amazing creations you'll invent in those closing seconds when you're sticking random eyes and flowers everywhere?

With such limited time to build in your mind will be totally focused, and that's just about the most joyful feeling there is.

Whatever you build, it's likely to be something unplanned because you have only 60 seconds to create something. Sometimes, we find joy unexpectedly amid the daily challenges we face. When we embrace those challenges, we often end up with something different from what we expected, yet something that makes us smile just the same.

Express yourself

Being grown up can involve a lot of putting on a brave face and generally not showing our emotions too much. Someone having a loud phone call in the restroom? It's not OK to rage at them and stomp on their phone. Even when you're feeling amazing, people don't always like it if you skip down the street singing. This isn't a Hollywood musical—though wouldn't it be fun if it were?

Children are really good at showing us what they think and feel, not just by living their emotions in front of us but also through activities such as painting, modeling clay, and building with LEGO bricks. And though we can't always express our emotions quite as much as we'd like to (wailing in the store when the last avocado has sold out is typically frowned upon), we all have the option of a LEGO session to give us the space we need to build how we're feeling.

Embrace your #currentmood and build something that helps you show exactly what you're feeling in this moment—and maybe your emotions at other times, too.

For example, what does "happy" look like to you? It could be bright colors, flowers, and pizzas, or something completely different—you'll find out when you start building. What does "how I feel at work" look like, or "I'm about to open my birthday presents"? Feel free to express your emotions and thoughts in any way you can build them.

Getting in touch with your emotions will help you tune in to which parts of your life make you feel a certain way that you may not have otherwise realized.

When you build to reveal or express your emotions, you'll get the satisfaction of making something that you can see and feel. Building a physical representation of your emotions can be the best way of acknowledging them and giving them the space in your life that they deserve.

We can't promise you won't feel rage over sold-out avocados ever again, but at least you'll be able to look forward to some cathartic building when you get home. And I always find that picking up my LEGO bricks—with their happy colors and shapes—makes me feel better.

Stack up your positivity

One of the first rules of adulting seems to be that you have to deal with lots of responsibilities all at once. It's all too easy to miss the individual moments of happiness that would take us back to a state of childlike joy. There's nothing like the big grin on a child's face, but there's no reason we can't have one, too — we just need to connect with the happy things that make us feel like a kid again.

 In order to get in touch with your inner child, spend a bit of LEGO playtime reconnecting with the little moments of joy that happen every day.

As you open your LEGO collection, let go of the worries of the day and start thinking about all the good things that have happened to you today. It could be something as small as "at least I didn't step on a LEGO brick" or something as big as "I got a new job."

Give a happy thought to each brick you pick up, and connect it to the ones before, until you have a new structure entirely built out of good things. It doesn't matter what your new LEGO build looks like—you may end up with a simple stack built out of all your happy thoughts.

The important thing to admire is all the happiness stored in those sweet bricks of goodness.

 Hold your new build in your hand and feel the happiness just bursting out of it—those are all your happy moments, stored in LEGO form.

Enjoy seeing just how many individual pieces of happiness have come together to make something new and unique—is that small blue brick the cup of coffee your colleague made for you, or the little bird you heard singing while you waited for the bus this morning? Each of those happy bricks has its own story to tell. And who knows, tomorrow may be even better!

One thing is for sure, a childlike grin will be on your face as you admire your simple, happy build.

Build Yourself Happy

8

The life-changing magic of tidying your LEGO® bricks

I know, I know, tidying up and putting away used to be the worst part of playtime. But hear me out. Clearing up after you've been playing with LEGO® bricks isn't an extra chore—it's part of the activity.

It's fun unboxing your LEGO bricks and spreading them out on your play space—and just as satisfying restoring order and tucking them neatly into their home again afterward. When you've packed your bricks away, leaving a smooth and uncluttered space where you were building, you'll feel a sense of calm from things being in their proper place.

 You may even be inspired to start sorting out other parts of your home, to continue benefiting from these positive feelings.

Once your LEGO pieces are back in their storage box, they'll be ready and waiting for you to make wonderful new creations with in your next session. One thing's for sure, if they're tucked away in a safe place, they won't turn up in your bed or anywhere else where small plastic bricks don't belong. And that is a surefire way to live a happier life, as I know from all-too-real experience.

The joy of tidying (your LEGO® bricks)

LEGO® playtime is an ideal form of self-care, giving us a chance to connect with all our senses and step away from the worries that buzz around us like pesky flies. It may not be Bikram yoga or a meditation retreat in a yurt, but playing with LEGO elements can give you many of the same happy-making benefits, and you don't normally have to bend into awkward positions to get them—unless you want to.

 So when you come to the end of a LEGO session, take a moment to appreciate the gift you've given yourself.

Then, when you're ready to start putting your bricks away, think about what you've achieved and the fun you've had making new creations. Snap the bricks apart, feeling that lovely clicky release of clutch power as each brick separates from its neighbor, and sort them in the way that suits you best.

If you're super-neat and organized, you may wish to sort your bricks into different colors or categories. If you're more of a "never mind the details, look at my stash" kind of person, you can have fun gathering up handfuls of pieces and funneling them into their container.

My favorite technique is what I call the "swoop scoop." I place the box under the edge of my LEGO table, then swoop my hand down and scoop the bricks off the edge of the table, where they fall noisily into their home. I love the waterfall-like sound they make as they cascade into my storage box. As each brick swoops by, I can remember how they all came together to help me relax, find happiness, and connect with friends and family.

 However you tidy your bricks, enjoy the process of organizing them and putting them away, and find a technique that pleases you.

Whether it's a dainty brick-by-brick style or more of an all at once method, do what feels right. And then give yourself a pat on the back for making "me time" and start looking forward to your next LEGO play session.

Storage techniques for any size of collection

Whether your LEGO collection is small enough to fit in the palm of your hand or so big that you've had to build an extra wing onto your house, you'll need somewhere to store your bricks, so they're neatly out of the way between sessions. Still, they'll need to be easy to get to when it's time to play again.

There are lots of storage options, and you can pick the one that works best for you. Here are some ideas to get you started:

- **Drawstring bag** that you can hang up on the back of a door, reminding you that LEGO fun is never far away. Just make sure it can close nice and tightly.

- **Craft box** with lots of separate compartments—the kind mechanics keep all their nuts and bolts in or crafters use for the tools of their trade.

- **Jam jar** or another container that's transparent so you can see your bricks even when they've been tidied. You'll also be saving the jam jar from the recycling bin. Everyone wins!

- **Cookie tin** that is no longer in use for its original purpose (clean out the crumbs first!). Some are beautifully designed and you'll be giving the cookie tin a new purpose, which is very eco-friendly!

Choose a container that brings you joy and gives your LEGO bricks a happy place to live when you're not using them. Keep it in sight, then you'll never forget to make time for LEGO fun.

But I want to keep it!

Brace yourself: it's time to get philosophical for a moment.

The truth is that not many things in life are permanent, and the path to happiness gets a little smoother when we accept that all the things we cling to (with our own type of emotional snapping power) might change, and we can't always do anything about it.

As in life, so in LEGO play . . . at the end of a session, we need to take our bricks apart, or else we wouldn't be able to make new things with them. Occasionally in this book I've suggested you might keep one of your builds for inspiration, but in general, LEGO bricks are meant to come apart at the end of each building session so they can go on to become another thing another day.

 So what can you do if you've had such a great LEGO time that you don't want to take your beautiful build apart into its separate bricks again?

A good way of preserving a build for the future is to take a photo of it—this is one of those times when smartphones can help with LEGO play, instead of diverting us away from our brickish joys.

You can save the photos of your creations in a special album, perfect for showing to friends and colleagues. ("Here's one I made earlier, and here's another one, and another—hang on, where are you going?")

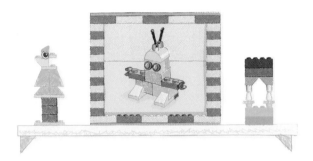

If you'd like to share your creations with a wider audience, you could post them to a social media account, for all friends and LEGO fans to enjoy. You never know who you might inspire to get building—and you might make some new friendships along the way as well.

All sorts of sorting

Time spent organizing your pieces gives you an opportunity to really get to know them, and sorting them can also be a great place to start if you don't know where to begin one of your models.

Here are some of the ways you can sort your pieces:

- **Group into matching colors.** You can make a new pile for each shade of a certain color or group all shades of one color together. The possibilities are endless!

- **Group into similar types.** Why not make piles of square bricks, flat tiles, special building blocks, and quirky pieces?

- **Group by size.** You could place all the biggest pieces at one end of your building space and all the smallest pieces at the other.

- **Group into "pieces I use all the time" and "pieces I don't use frequently."** Or any other grouping that occurs to you.

When you look at your bricks in these different ways, new combinations will suggest themselves to you. Try building with pieces of one color or category. Or perhaps take one piece from each group. Whatever you choose, your imagination will be stretched in new ways.

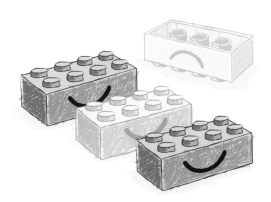

Build Yourself Happy

9

Keep calm and carry LEGO® bricks

Now that you've (re)discovered the joy of LEGO® building, you'll want to carry its happiness wherever you go. Your regular play space at home will probably always be Brick HQ for you, but wouldn't it be great if you could enjoy the experience of playing with LEGO elements when you're out and about as well? After all, you've got coffee and a snack to go—a handful of bricks is just as portable as those.

While you won't be able to use your whole collection when you're on the road or away from your home, there are lots of ways you can still enjoy playing with LEGO bricks. Once you start thinking creatively, you'll see just how far your little bricks can take you, whether you're at work, waiting for a bus, or even having a picnic under a shady tree. With some traveling LEGO stash help, you'll be sure to keep feeling happy wherever you go.

Carrying LEGO® joy into your daily life

Despite centuries of technological improvements, there are still public places with no space for LEGO® play—I'm not sure how this hasn't been fixed yet, but until all buses, cafés, and workplaces have a LEGO play space, we're going to have to find some other ways to keep the LEGO joy going when we're on the move.

The simplest of all LEGO talismans is the "single brick." I like to use a classic 2x4 brick, as it fits nicely in my hand and I can still find it in my coat pocket among the candy wrappers and old receipts.

By keeping a LEGO brick in your pocket, you'll always have a mini stress-buster on hand. If you have an important meeting coming up or are running late, the sensory experience of feeling the nubbly studs on the bricks can help release tension.

Concentrate your thoughts on the sensations of the bricks, and allow yourself to imagine your next building session as you beam yourself (mentally at least) to your LEGO happy place.

 Just one brick can stimulate your imagination with lots of ideas for your next LEGO session.

The simplest build

The smallest possible LEGO kit is two bricks. Every coat pocket has space for a couple of bricks, so you never need to be without that oh-so-pleasing clutch power. Whether you're sitting at your desk, waiting at a bus stop, or having coffee in the local café, you can take clutch power with you!

Whichever two pieces you choose, you'll find when you start to connect them that there are lots of different ways they can fit together. Perhaps they could stack perfectly on top of each other, or maybe one brick could stick out above or below the other one. When you rotate one of your bricks, you'll find even more ways to connect them. If you connect them with just one stud, you might find they are precariously balanced. The more studs you can use to connect things, the more solid a structure you will end up with.

You see—even two bricks can give a great range of options, and engage your mind when you'd otherwise have the mental equivalent of a screen saver.

You can enjoy your two-brick connections for exactly what they are—two pieces, securely held together until you pull them apart. Or you can use each different configuration as the starting point in your mind for a new idea.

Are they the foundation of a wall, the base of a figure, an arm, or part of a vehicle chassis, for example?

With this in mind, you can start planning what you're going to build later. Or simply enjoy being in this moment and appreciate the actions that you're doing.

 Your teeny tiny mini LEGO kit will give you all the fun of building while you're out and about—and it's certain to bring a burst of extra joy to your day.

On-the-go kit

If you've got a vacation or work trip coming up, you don't have to leave all your LEGO fun at home. With a small collection of LEGO bricks in your carry-on bag, you can take the happiness of LEGO building on the road.

If you don't want to sound like a human maraca as you walk down the street, it's probably best to use a small bag, a pencil case, or a zippered makeup bag to hold your stash. (Though if you do have that giveaway LEGO shake-it-all-about sound as you walk down the street, you will be easier to identify by fellow LEGO fans.)

You'll be amazed by how many things you can build with a small selection of pieces. If you're a careful kind of person who likes to plan everything to the last stud, you can curate a special collection of traveling pieces. If, on the other, hand you're more of a grab-and-go person, a random handful from your main stash will be just as good, and may yield very unusual results.

 With a small travel bag of LEGO bricks, you'll be able to enjoy building all the time.

Thinking with bricks

LEGO bricks are for playing—and playing is for everyone. Having a playful approach to life is good for us in so many ways, and it stops us falling into a rut and forgetting to stay open to new experiences.

But there is more to LEGO bricks than playing. Did you know that the LEGO system, as well as being fabulous to play with, can also help you think?

At the LEGO head offices in Denmark, the majority of meeting rooms are equipped with bowls of LEGO bricks, and people are encouraged to play with them during discussions because they've found that it helps with concentration. In a way, it's a lot like doodling. Many people find that thoughts flow more easily when they have a pen in their hand to idly create pictures and patterns with.

The next time you have some thinking to do, why not take a handful of LEGO pieces to play with? You may find that making connections between bricks helps you subconsciously connect ideas, too.

Perhaps by the time you have finished your creation, you will have come up with a complete plan for some upcoming project. And if it works for you, you could try introducing the "doodling with LEGO bricks" concept into your next meeting at work. After all, there's no reason why meetings need to be pen and paper only, and if some little blocks of happiness can help them go more smoothly, what's not to like?

Draw your models

You can't always be near your bricks (boo!) but you can always be thinking about building (yay!). If you don't have access to any bricks, you can still think about what you're going to make in your next LEGO session. You may be in a long meeting, on a flight, or waiting to get through to someone on the phone, but if you can't keep your hands busy building, you can grab a notebook or a piece of scrap paper and start sketching out ideas for your next build.

Your drawings don't have to be exactly lifelike or perfect blueprints—all that matters is that they should capture an idea in a way that fires your imagination. And simply thinking about bricks and all the fun you can have with them will increase your joy factor hugely (especially if you've been number one in the hold queue for at least 20 minutes).

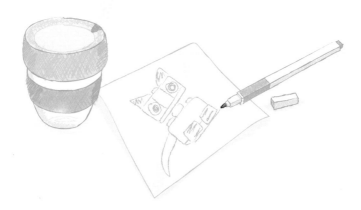

If you're in a situation where drawing is frowned upon or impractical, you can put your mental architect to work instead, drawing up a Leonardo da Vinci–style plan in your mind, ready to bring to bricky life when you're back at your LEGO station again.

 No matter where you are or where you're going, there are endless ways to play with LEGO bricks to help you feel more relaxed and realize the simplest joys in your life.

Build Yourself Happy

10

A little extra inspiration

A quick guide to LEGO® terminology

Let's take a look at some of the most common LEGO® elements.

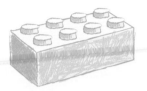

Bricks: These timeless building blocks are the basis of most LEGO builds. They come in many shapes and sizes.

Plates: Each flat, stud-topped element is useful for adding subtle changes in height to your build. Larger plates are useful foundations for bigger-scale builds. Three plates stacked together have the same height as one brick.

Tiles: Tiles are similar to plates, but with no studs on top. This gives them a smooth look for more realistic builds.

Brick separator: This handy lever comes to the rescue whenever two of your bricks decide they want to stay together forever. Truly life-changing!

Minifigures and accessories: These friendly characters have been with us since 1978, piloting LEGO vehicles and living in LEGO homes. They also come with pretty cool extras—because some minifigures enjoy the occasional glass of wine or have hobbies such as photography, just like non-plastic people.

Special elements: There are plenty of LEGO elements, such as wheels, connectors, LEGO flora, and more that don't fit neatly into any of the aforementioned categories. But that doesn't mean that these elements can't add a special touch to your builds.

Model ideas

By now you'll know there's no better way to stretch your creativity than by going with the flow and building without anything particular in mind. But some days you may feel like you need a springboard for your build ideas. Here are some simple and playful models to inspire you and get you started.

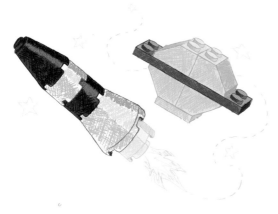

● **Rocket and planet:**
Just a handful of bricks can take you out of this world.

● **Cute robot:**
Want to reboot your brain? Think high-tech with a mini bot.

Toy on wheels:
Build a cool structure,
add wheels, and get
set for a joyful spin.

Tree and bird:
Create a calm mini
space with a simple
tree and a tiny bird.

● **Mash-up models:**
Try mixing two ideas
together for an
unusual twist.

● **Dream home:**
Build your happy place with
colorful, classic bricks.

● **Scrumptious snacks:**
With just a few bricks you can
make delicious-looking treats.

● **Perfect pet:**
Want a problem-free pet?
Build yourself a cute and
quirky companion.

Afterword

Now that you've reached the end of this book, you will have discovered a variety of simple ways to weave play into your otherwise busy and demanding life and reaped the benefits that creative building can bring. Give yourself a pat on the back!

You will have got to know your LEGO bricks; their many shapes, textures, and colors; and the wonderful sensory experience that can be a great aid to contemplation and relaxation.

Perhaps you've thrown caution to the wind, experimenting with different builds without any pressure to perform.

 Maybe you've been able to reset your mind into a more relaxed, creative mode, helping you develop more positive approaches to life's challenges.

On the way you will have boosted your mood by visualizing and building your happiest places and dreams, helping you see your ambitions and way forward in a clearer way.

And let's not forget the fun and silliness to be had while sharing LEGO playtime with your friends and the incredible connections and innovative builds you've created in the process.

Some LEGO building activities will resonate with you more than others. Once you've found your favorite—the one that really works for you—it can be the first thing you reach for to lift your spirits, inspire your creativity, or help you drift off to sleep. But if you get out of the routine, it's easy to refer back to the pages of this book for a quick building fix, just when you feel like it.

I hope that through reading this book and discovering the playful possibilities of LEGO bricks you've found a way to bring more color, relaxation, and creativity into your life. And that your long journey into the magical world of LEGO fun continues to be ever rewarding.
Go ahead, build yourself happy!

Sources

Here are some of the studies referenced in this book. Check out these sources for more information:

Pages 12–13: LEGO® Foundation, The. (2018), *Skills for holistic development.*

https://www.legofoundation.com/en/why-play/skills-for-holistic-development

Page 17: LEGO® Foundation, The. (2018). LEGO® *Play Well Report 2018.*

https://www.lego.com/en-us/aboutus/news-room/2018/august/play-well-report

Page 38: UCL News. (2019). *Creative activities help the brain to cope with emotions.*

https://www.ucl.ac.uk/news/2019/may/creative-activities-help-brain-cope-emotions

Page 54: Tchounwou, Paul B. (ed.). (2015). Autonomic Nervous System Responses to Viewing Green and Built Settings: Differentiating Between Sympathetic and Parasympathetic Activity. *International Journal of Environmental Research and Public Health.*

https://www.ncbi.nlm.nih.gov/pmc/articles/PMC4690962/

Pages 79–81: The National Sleep Foundation. "How to Design the Perfect Bedtime Routine."

https://www.sleep.org/articles/design-perfect-bedtime-routine/

About the author

Abbie Headon studied music at the University of Oxford and currently works as an editor and writer. She has written several books, including *The Power of Yes, The Power of No, Poetry First Aid Kit,* and *Literary First Aid Kit*.

In her free time Abbie likes reading, cooking, avoiding exercise, spending time with friends, visiting historic places, and watching YouTube documentaries about Japan.

Abbie first started playing with LEGO® bricks as a child and especially loved the LEGO® Space theme. She moved on to LEGO® Technic and had a really cool set with a motor unit. However, when she grew up she got distracted by work and other boring grown up things, and let her LEGO habit fade away. Abbie has loved rediscovering the joy of LEGO play as an adult, and now has a number of sets on her wish list for next Christmas. When she's playing with LEGO bricks, she enjoys just pottering and finding out what her builds will be, brick by brick.

Her favorite element is the little orange fish but she also loves the classic chunky 2x4 brick because, with enough of those, you can build anything!

Abbie lives in Portsmouth, England, and loves being by the seaside.

Find her online at: www.abbieheadon.com
Follow her on Twitter: @abbieheadon
Follow her on Instagram: @abbieheadon

If you've loved the activities and building ideas in this book and want more inspiration for what to build next, check out these LEGO® books from DK!

Create amazing models with tips and ideas that unlock the secrets of great LEGO building

Spark new play ideas with story-themed chapters

Discover building ideas from LEGO fan builders to suit all abilities and ages

Be inspired every day of the year with 365 things to do with LEGO bricks

Senior Editor Tori Kosara
Project Art Editor Jenny Edwards
Pre-production Producer Siu Yin Chan
Senior Producer Lloyd Robertson
Managing Editor Paula Regan
Managing Art Editor Jo Connor
Publisher Julie Ferris
Art Director Lisa Lanzarini

Jacket illustrations and design Jenny Edwards

Dorling Kindersley would like to thank Randi Sørensen, Heidi K. Jensen, Paul Hansford,
and Martin Leighton Lindhardt at the LEGO Group; Julia March and Selina Wood for
editorial assistance and Megan Douglass at DK for Americanizing.

First American Edition, 2019
Published in the United States by DK Publishing
1450 Broadway, Suite 801, New York, New York 10018

A WORLD OF IDEAS:
SEE ALL THERE IS TO KNOW

www.dk.com
www.LEGO.com